CROCODILES

Maddie Gibbs

PowerKiDS press™

New York

Published in 2011 by The Rosen Publishing Group, Inc.
29 East 21st Street, New York, NY 10010

First Edition

Editor: Amelie von Zumbusch
Layout Design: Greg Tucker

Photo Credits: Cover Tom Brakefield/Stockbyte/Thinkstock; pp. 4–5, 11, 13, 19, 21, 24 (top right), 24 (bottom left) Shutterstock.com; p. 7 Jupiterimages/Photos.com/Thinkstock; pp. 9, 24 (bottom right) Anup Shah/Digital Vision/Thinkstock; pp. 15, 23, 24 (top left) iStockphoto/Thinkstock; p. 17 Jupiterimages/Photos.com/Thinkstock.

Library of Congress Cataloging-in-Publication Data

Gibbs, Maddie.
 Crocodiles / Maddie Gibbs. — 1st ed.
     p. cm. — (Safari animals)
 Includes index.
 ISBN 978-1-4488-2504-2 (library binding) — ISBN 978-1-4488-2594-3 (pbk.) —
ISBN 978-1-4488-2595-0 (6-pack)
 1. Crocodiles—Juvenile literature. I. Title.
 QL666.C925G535 2011
 597.98'2—dc22

                              2010018389

Manufactured in the United States of America

CPSIA Compliance Information: Batch #WW11PK: For Further Information contact Rosen Publishing, New York, New York at 1-800-237-9932

CONTENTS

People go on safaris to look at animals. You can see crocodiles on safaris!

4

These are Nile crocodiles.
They live in Africa's lakes
and rivers.

Crocodiles are hunters. They have sharp **teeth**.

Crocodiles creep up on their food. Then they catch it with their teeth.

Crocodiles have **scales**. This helps keep them safe from other hunters.

When they are cold, crocodiles **bask** in the sun to warm up.

When it is hot, crocodiles dive into the water. They are good swimmers. They swim a lot.

Baby crocodiles are known as hatchlings. This is because they **hatch** from eggs.

Mother crocodiles care for their hatchlings. This baby is riding on its mother's back.

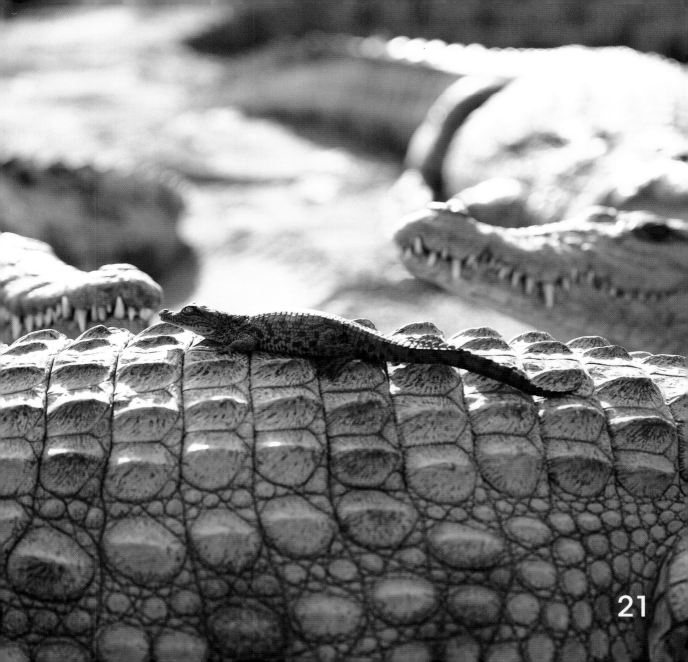

Young crocodiles grow fast. In their first year, they grow about 1 foot (30 cm).

Words to Know

bask

hatch

scales

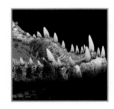

teeth

Web Sites

Due to the changing nature of Internet links, PowerKids Press has developed an online list of Web sites related to the subject of this book. This site is updated regularly. Please use this link to access the list:
www.powerkidslinks.com/safari/croc/